GROUNDBREAKING WOMEN IN POLITICS

KAMALA HARRIS

by Kelsey Jopp

FOCUS
READERS.

VOYAGER

www.focusreaders.com

Focus Readers is distributed by North Star Editions:
sales@northstareditions.com | 888-417-0195

Produced for Focus Readers by Red Line Editorial.

Content Consultant: Christina Bejarano, Professor of Multicultural Women's and Gender Studies, Texas Woman's University

Photographs ©: John Locher/AP Images, cover, 1; Joshua Roberts/Reuters/Newscom, 4–5; J. Scott Applewhite/AP Images, 7; Sundry Photography/Shutterstock Images, 8–9; Ernest K. Bennett/AP Images, 11; Eric Glenn/Shutterstock Images, 13; Mary F. Calvert/The Mercury News/MediaNews Group/Getty Images, 14–15; Spondylolithesis/iStockphoto, 17; Red Line Editorial, 19, 33; felipe caparros/Shutterstock Images, 21; Ben Margot/Shutterstock Images, 22–23; Rich Pedroncelli/AP Images, 25; Jeff Chiu/AP Images, 27; Joe Ravi/Shutterstock Images, 28–29; Ringo H.W. Chiu/AP Images, 31; Andrew Harnik/AP Images, 34–35; mark reinstein/Shutterstock Images, 37; United States Senate, 39; Monkey Business Images/Shutterstock Images, 41; Kim Wilson/Shutterstock Images, 42–43; Paul Sancya/AP Images, 45

Library of Congress Cataloging-in-Publication Data
Library of Congress Cataloging-in-Publication Data is available on the Library of Congress website.

ISBN
978-1-64493-088-5 (hardcover)
978-1-64493-167-7 (paperback)
978-1-64493-325-1 (ebook pdf)
978-1-64493-246-9 (hosted ebook)

Printed in the United States of America
Mankato, MN
012020

ABOUT THE AUTHOR

Kelsey Jopp is an editor, writer, and lifelong learner. She lives in Saint Paul, Minnesota, where she enjoys practicing yoga and playing endless fetch with her sheltie, Teddy.

TABLE OF CONTENTS

CHAPTER 1

INTERROGATION

In January 2017, Kamala Harris joined the US Senate. She was one of 15 senators on the Select Committee on Intelligence. This group oversees the agencies that gather information for the US government. That June, the committee held a hearing. Harris and the other senators questioned Attorney General Jeff Sessions.

As attorney general, Sessions served as the head lawyer for the US government.

Kamala Harris was sworn in to the US Senate on January 3, 2017.

Sessions was also one of President Donald Trump's earliest supporters. He advised Trump's election campaign.

In July 2016, the Federal Bureau of Investigation (FBI) began looking into Trump's campaign. The FBI thought campaign officials might have been in contact with the Russian government. The FBI feared the two groups were working together to sway the election. After Trump won in November 2016, this fear grew.

In January 2017, Sessions said he had no contact with Russia during the campaign. He made this statement **under oath**. But in March, news spread that Sessions had met with a Russian official twice. In the June hearing, the committee wanted answers.

Each senator had only five minutes to question Sessions. Harris focused her time on one issue.

Harris questions Attorney General Jeff Sessions during a hearing in June 2017.

She wanted notes from Sessions's meetings with the Russian official. Sessions struggled to answer Harris's questions. He said her quick questions made him nervous. But Harris was a former **prosecutor**. She did not back down. She pressed Sessions for the full five minutes. Afterward, the hearing received a lot of news attention. Harris had served in the Senate for only six months. But she was already seen as a rising political star.

CHAPTER 2

RAISED IN COMMUNITY

Kamala Harris was born in Oakland, California, on October 20, 1964. Her father, Donald, was a professor of economics. Her mother, Shyamala, researched breast cancer. Both of Kamala's parents had immigrated to the United States. Her father was from Jamaica, and her mother was from India. Kamala's sister, Maya, was born in 1967. The Harris family found a sense of home in Oakland's black and Indian communities.

The city of Oakland is in northern California's Bay Area, along with San Francisco and San Jose.

In the 1960s, Kamala's parents marched in the **civil rights movement**. They were protesting racial **discrimination** in the United States. Sometimes, they brought Kamala along in a stroller. Even as a baby, Kamala was exposed to the world of political activism.

Growing up, Kamala was also involved in Oakland's black community. Her family lived in mostly black neighborhoods. Kamala made friends with many other black children. On the weekends, Kamala and her family worshipped at a black Baptist church.

Surrounded by black culture, Kamala grew up with confidence about her race. Her mother also exposed Kamala and Maya to their Indian heritage. The girls ate Indian food and wore Indian jewelry. They visited Hindu temples, too. The family visited relatives in India and Jamaica.

△ The Black Panthers formed in Oakland during the 1960s. This political group worked for black people's civil rights.

In these ways, Kamala learned to embrace her biracial identity.

Kamala's parents divorced when she was seven years old. Five years later, Kamala moved to Quebec, Canada, with her mother and sister. Here, Kamala learned to speak French. She even organized her first protest. She and her sister protested a policy at their apartment building. The policy banned children from playing on the lawn. Kamala and her sister won.

In middle school and high school, Kamala became involved in many activities, including music and dance. Though she was young, Kamala knew what she wanted to do with her life. Her dream was to become a lawyer.

After high school, Kamala Harris headed to Washington, DC. She attended Howard University. Howard was a historically black college. The school had many well-known graduates, including Thurgood Marshall. Marshall was a lawyer who became the first black justice on the US Supreme Court in 1967. He had been one of Harris's heroes from a young age.

➤ THINK ABOUT IT

Harris was raised with a focus on community. How do you think this affected her career? What qualities and interests did she develop?

▲ Howard University was founded in 1867.

At Howard, Harris became involved in politics. On weekends, she protested South African apartheid. Apartheid was a system of racial segregation. The South African government was separating people from one another based on their race. In 1986, she graduated with a degree in political science and economics. Afterward, she attended Hastings College of the Law back in California. She graduated in 1989 and became a lawyer. She had made her dream come true.

CHAPTER 3

SMART ON CRIME

After law school, Kamala Harris became a prosecutor. Many of her family and friends were surprised. They thought she would become a civil rights lawyer. But Harris felt she could make greater change in law enforcement. Growing up, Harris saw how law enforcement affected communities of color. Prosecutors can decide which crimes are more important than others. In addition, they can choose whom to focus on.

In the 1990s, Kamala Harris worked as a deputy district attorney in Oakland, California.

Harris could also decide prison sentences and **rehabilitation** options. For example, drug-related crimes are common. Harris could send those offenders to rehab instead of prison. Rehab provides treatment to people struggling with drug use. This type of treatment often makes people less likely to **reoffend**.

Harris also chose this role so that she could stand up for victims. In 1990, Harris took her first job as a prosecutor. She handled murder, robbery, and sexual assault cases. Many victims of sexual assault were women and children. In these cases, Harris often dealt tough sentences.

Harris held that job for eight years. Then she moved to the San Francisco District Attorney's Office. After two more years, she switched to the San Francisco City Attorney's Office. She led the Division on Families and Children. There, Harris

▲ Harris worked in San Francisco's City Hall.

started a program that helped emergency room staff recognize cases of child sexual abuse. She also pushed for stronger laws against this abuse.

In 2003, Harris was elected district attorney of San Francisco. She was the first woman, black person, and South Asian American to hold the position. Harris used the role to take greater action against crime. One of her goals was to reduce the rate of people who reoffend.

To meet that goal, Harris founded Back on Track. This program gave offenders training in life skills and job seeking. It was open to people who committed nonviolent, drug-related crimes. They could attend the program instead of prison. Back on Track was a success. After two years, only 10 percent of participants had reoffended. Normally, more than 50 percent of drug offenders in California reoffend. The program was cheaper than prison, too. It saved the taxpayers money.

Harris tried to prevent crime in other ways. For example, she focused on school attendance as a way to prevent murders. In San Francisco, 94 percent of murder victims younger than 25 had not finished high school. High school dropouts often had low attendance in elementary school. In response, Harris started programs to help parents improve their children's attendance. If a child's attendance did not improve, the parent could be charged with a crime.

As district attorney, Harris showed that fighting crime takes creativity. Many prosecutors only reacted to crime. But for Harris, preventing crime was just as important. She came up with new approaches to hard issues.

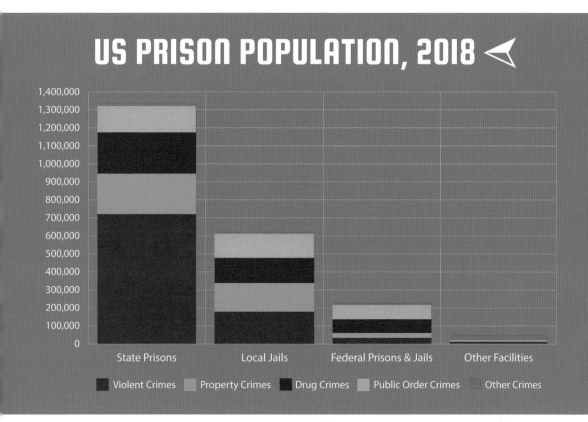

US PRISON POPULATION, 2018 ◁

| | Violent Crimes | Property Crimes | Drug Crimes | Public Order Crimes | Other Crimes |

CRIME

Kamala Harris was a prosecutor for 20 years. This experience made her an expert on crime. She developed strong views on the topic. She wanted to change much of the **criminal justice system**.

Many times, Harris stuck to her views. For example, she often spoke out against the death penalty. She did not think anyone should be sentenced to death. In 2004, her stance was tested. That year, a gang member killed a police officer. Many people, including California police, demanded a death sentence. But Harris stood her ground. She refused to seek a death sentence in the case. Harris's decision hurt her relationship with the California police. She lost the support of many politicians and voters. Even so, she proved that she could be firm under pressure.

Harris was also willing to make tough convictions. As district attorney, she more than

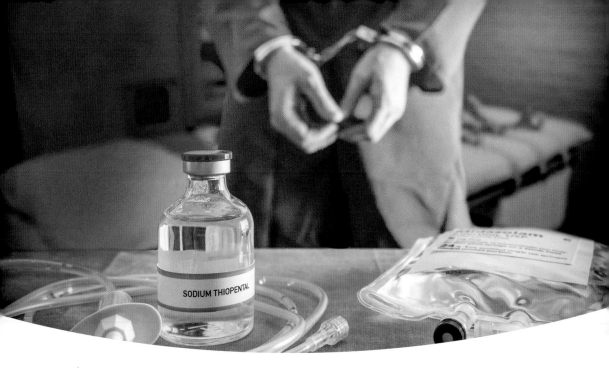

Since 1973, more than 160 people in the United States were sentenced to death for crimes they did not commit.

doubled conviction rates for gun **felonies**. Her office also increased the number of violent offenders put behind bars.

In 2009, Harris published a book called *Smart on Crime*. In the book, she presented her ideas on how to reduce crime. For example, she wanted to stop ex-offenders from reoffending. In her mind, smart action against crime required balance. It took not only tough sentences but creative problem-solving as well.

CHAPTER 4

CALIFORNIA ATTORNEY GENERAL

On November 12, 2008, Kamala Harris announced she was running for attorney general of California. The attorney general is the state's top lawyer. California is also the US state with the largest population. That fact made the position all the more important. If Harris won, she could help many people.

Harris was running against Steve Cooley. He was serving as Los Angeles's district attorney.

Kamala Harris enters San Francisco's City Hall to declare her run for California attorney general.

Cooley belonged to the Republican Party. Republicans tend to favor more conservative stances. They support established social values. Harris was a member of the Democratic Party. Democrats tend to favor progressive changes. They push for more social freedoms.

On November 2, 2010, California voters headed to the polls. By the end of the night, Cooley seemed to have won. However, cities still had to count votes that were mailed in. By November 25, the results were clear. Harris had won. She became California's first female attorney general.

As attorney general, Harris's stances varied. She sometimes supported progressive policies. For example, Harris launched implicit bias training for police officers. Bias occurs when a person judges others based on race, gender, or other factors. Implicit bias happens when someone

Harris debates Steve Cooley during the race for California attorney general in 2010.

judges without thinking about it. This type of bias causes officers to arrest people of color more often than white people. Harris's training taught officers to be aware of their biases. It stressed the importance of fair law enforcement.

At other times, Harris chose not to support progressive policies. She stayed silent on proposals to reduce punishments for nonviolent crimes. She also opposed a **bill** that would have forced the state to look into shootings by police.

In addition, Harris defended the death penalty. Personally, she was against this punishment. But as attorney general, she decided to allow it. She did not want to let her voters down.

For Republicans, Harris was too progressive. For many Democrats, she was not progressive enough. Still, Harris tried to make smart decisions in office. In 2011, she was involved in a case against mortgage lenders. These lenders were banks that helped people pay for their homes. President Barack Obama wanted Harris to settle the case. By settling, the lenders would pay a certain fee. Then the case would be over. But Harris wanted a better deal. She looked further

> **THINK ABOUT IT**

Harris's decisions on certain issues were sometimes at odds with one another. Why do you think this was?

Harris listens to a victim of mortgage fraud during a 2011 hearing.

into the state's side of the case. In the end, her decision paid off. California homeowners received a much higher amount than the original offer.

In 2012, Harris spoke at the Democratic National Convention. She had already been noticed as a rising talent. After all, she had proved herself in court again and again. Harris's speech brought her more attention. Many Democrats agreed that she had a bright future in politics.

CHAPTER 5

A SEAT IN THE SENATE

By 2015, Kamala Harris had her eyes on the US Senate. Together, the Senate and the House of Representatives make up the US Congress. They create US laws. Of the two, the Senate is considered the upper house. It has only 100 members. A senator's term lasts six years. As a result, securing a Senate seat can be difficult. In addition, California's two Senate seats had been held by the same people for more than 20 years.

The US Senate and House of Representatives are both located in the Capitol Building.

In January 2015, however, Senator Barbara Boxer announced that she would not be running for reelection. One of California's Senate seats was finally open. Within a week, Harris announced her campaign. More than 30 others joined the race.

The final two candidates were Harris and Loretta Sanchez. Sanchez was a member of the US House of Representatives. She was also a Democrat. However, the two women focused on different issues. Harris promised to raise the minimum wage. She also spoke about immigration and the criminal justice system. In contrast, Sanchez focused on the military and veterans' affairs.

For much of the race, Harris was ahead in the polls. She had the support of several politicians, including President Obama. The election results were no surprise. On November 8, 2016, Harris

 Kamala Harris gives a speech during her 2016 run for US Senate.

won with 62 percent of votes. She became the state's first woman of color in the Senate. She was also the country's first Indian American senator.

Once in the Senate, Harris made decisions that surprised political observers. For instance, she wrote a bill to get rid of cash bail. Bail releases **defendants** from jail until their trials. However, some defendants cannot afford bail. And trials can take months, or sometimes years, to happen.

As a result, many low-income people spend unnecessary time in jail simply because they cannot afford bail. Like many Democrats, Harris thought this was wrong. But before joining the Senate, her stance was not as clear. As attorney general, she had stayed silent on the issue.

Harris's shift on this issue raised alarm. Critics questioned Harris's true beliefs. They thought she was trying to appear more progressive than she was. After all, as a lawyer, Harris had not been that progressive. She had opposed several changes to the criminal justice system.

Harris was not the only one to change her mind. Public opinion had also shifted. From the 1970s to 1990s, violent crime rates rose. News coverage of drug use also rose. More of the public wanted a tougher response to crime. As a result, the US prison population rose by large numbers.

By the 2000s, opinions about the criminal justice system had changed again. Many activists argued that the system was racist. They pushed for change. Perhaps Harris's stance changed in response. But her critics worried she was simply saying what the public wanted to hear.

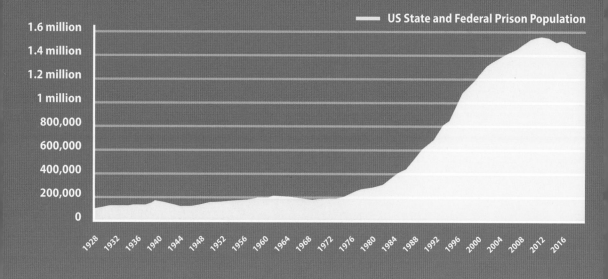

US PRISON POPULATION GROWTH ◁

As of 2017, the United States housed more prisoners than any other country.

US State and Federal Prison Population

CHAPTER 6

TAKING A STAND

After her election to the Senate, Kamala Harris joined several committees. Committees play a large role in the Senate. They allow senators to build deeper knowledge in certain areas. Committee members can then advise the rest of the Senate on what actions to take.

Each party in the Senate is responsible for committee assignments. The Democratic Party assigned Harris to serve on four committees.

In 2017, former FBI head James Comey testified before the Senate Intelligence Committee.

Harris joined committees on the federal budget, security, the justice system, and intelligence.

Harris's committee work brought her important opportunities. In her first year, she participated in high-profile hearings. In these hearings, Harris used her legal experience to question witnesses. When witnesses avoided her questions, she pressed them further.

In June 2017, she questioned Deputy Attorney General Rod Rosenstein. The next week, she questioned Attorney General Jeff Sessions. These hearings were part of the investigation into Russian interference in the 2016 presidential election. However, in both hearings, Republican senators interrupted Harris's questioning. They said Harris wouldn't let the witnesses answer. Some senators defended Harris. They claimed she was interrupted more often than white, male

Attorney General Jeff Sessions answers questions before the Senate Intelligence Committee in June 2017.

senators. Harris did not let the criticism stop her. She kept asking tough questions during hearings.

Aside from her committee work, Harris worked to pass new laws. She sponsored, or introduced, dozens of bills. However, most of Harris's bills did not become law. They failed to pass through Congress. When Harris first joined the Senate, Republicans controlled both houses of Congress. And after the 2018 elections, Republicans still controlled the Senate.

As of 2019, only four of Harris's bills had become law. Two of the laws had to do with natural disasters, such as hurricanes. One bill increased support for the victims of disasters. The other changed how disaster death tolls were counted. Harris's other successful bills preserved parts of California history. For example, one bill set aside land for a historic site.

Harris's unsuccessful bills touched on a variety of issues. She introduced bills in the areas of crime, veterans' affairs, and more. Many of her bills focused on communities in need. She especially wanted to support working families.

➤ THINK ABOUT IT

Harris struggled to move her bills through Congress. Why do you think this was? What barriers might she have faced?

Senators meet in the Senate chamber to vote for bills.

In 2017, more than half of Americans could not afford an unexpected $500 expense. In 2018, Harris introduced a bill to solve this problem. Under the bill, families in need would receive $500 per month. Harris also put forward the Rent Relief Act. This bill would provide financial help to low-income renters. These bills failed to pass through Congress in 2018. However, Harris introduced both bills again in 2019. She was dedicated to helping those who needed it most.

WOMEN AND PEOPLE OF COLOR

Growing up, Kamala Harris witnessed many struggles in her community. She saw single mothers trying to support families. She saw black youth treated unfairly by police. And she saw immigrants fall into poverty. When she grew older, she wanted to help these people. She wanted to be a voice for women and people of color. That way, she could help find solutions.

As a prosecutor, Harris put her plan into action. She dealt tough sentences to people who abused women and children. And she formed rehabilitation programs for nonviolent offenders. These programs aimed to break cycles of crime in black communities.

As a senator, Harris continued doing this important work. In 2018, she introduced a bill that

△ Black women die from pregnancy-related causes at three times the rate of white women.

would recognize Black Maternal Health Week. In the United States, black women face higher-risk pregnancies than white women. That same year, Harris also introduced the Maternal CARE Act. This bill aimed to improve the quality of care for all pregnant women.

Harris knew that one area of focus was not enough. So she tried to make changes in crime, health, and other areas. That way, she could reach as many women and people of color as possible.

TEXT FEARLESS
TO 70785
KAMALAHARRIS.ORG

CHAPTER 7

LOOKING AHEAD

After more than two years in the Senate, Kamala Harris had become a household name. High-profile hearings had brought her more attention. In 2018, she questioned Brett Kavanaugh. He was a Supreme Court nominee accused of sexual assault. In 2019, she also questioned Attorney General William Barr. She pressed him on his role in the Russia investigation.

Kamala Harris announces her candidacy for president in Oakland, California.

On January 21, 2019, Harris made a major announcement. She was running for president in the 2020 election. For years, Harris had spoken out against President Donald Trump. She disagreed with his decisions on immigration and transgender rights. She also condemned Trump's neglect of communities of color. She believed the United States needed a new president. And she was confident she was fit for the job.

Harris was running against more than 20 other Democrats. Of the senators in the race, Harris had one of the lowest approval ratings. In California, 68 percent of voters approved of Harris. Meanwhile, Senator Bernie Sanders held a 92 percent approval rating in Vermont. Still, Harris received a great deal of media attention.

Harris stood out in more ways than one. Many Americans respected the strength she showed

△ Harris speaks during a Democratic primary debate in July 2019.

during hearings. They also thought Harris represented important communities. She was a woman of color and relatively young. For many, she represented the future of the Democratic Party. And Harris was determined to continue serving Americans, no matter her title.

FOCUS ON
KAMALA HARRIS

Write your answers on a separate piece of paper.

1. Write a paragraph that describes the main ideas of Chapter 4.

2. In the Senate, Harris has served on committees and introduced bills. Which of these roles do you think she was most successful in? Why?

3. Which office was Harris elected to in 2010?
   - **A.** San Francisco District Attorney's Office
   - **B.** Attorney General of California
   - **C.** US Senator from California

4. Before Harris was elected to the US Senate, why had California's two seats been filled for more than 20 years?
   - **A.** The senators served a standard term of 24 years.
   - **B.** The senators were reelected several times.
   - **C.** The senators refused to give up their positions.

Answer key on page 48.

GLOSSARY

bill
A written plan to create or change a law.

civil rights movement
A mass struggle against racial discrimination in the United States in the 1950s and 1960s.

criminal justice system
The system of rules, processes, and agencies that manage crime and enforce an area's laws.

defendants
Individuals who have been accused of committing a crime by a court of law.

discrimination
Unfair treatment of a person or group based on race, gender, or other factors.

felonies
Crimes that the government considers serious, often punishable by time in prison.

prosecutor
A lawyer who conducts a case against a defendant in a criminal court.

rehabilitation
The process of returning to normal life, behavior, or activity.

reoffend
To commit another crime after serving time for a previous crime.

under oath
Having formally sworn to tell the truth in a legal context.

TO LEARN MORE

BOOKS

Campbell, Janis, and Catherine Collison. *Kamala Harris.* New York: Lucent Press, 2019.

Harris, Kamala. *The Truths We Hold: An American Journey (Young Readers Edition)*. New York: Philomel Books, 2019.

Lanser, Amanda. *Women in Politics and Government.* Minneapolis: Abdo Publishing, 2017.

NOTE TO EDUCATORS

Visit **www.focusreaders.com** to find lesson plans, activities, links, and other resources related to this title.

INDEX

Answer Key: 1. Answers will vary; **2.** Answers will vary; **3.** B; **4.** B